HIDDEN HISTORY
SPIES

Nathan Hale

AMERICA'S FIRST SPY

by Aaron Derr
illustrated by Tami Wicinas

RED
CHAIR
•PRESS•

Hidden History: Spies is produced and published by Red Chair Press:
Red Chair Press LLC   PO Box 333   South Egremont, MA 01258-0333
www.redchairpress.com

Publisher's Cataloging-In-Publication Data
Names: Derr, Aaron. | Wicinas, Tami, illustrator.
Title: Nathan Hale : America's first spy / by Aaron Derr ; illustrated by Tami Wicinas.

Description: [South Egremont, Massachusetts] : Red Chair Press, [2018] | Series: Hidden
history: spies | Interest age level: 008-012. | Includes sidebars of interest, a glossary, and
resources to learn more. | Includes bibliographical references and index. | Summary:
"It was September 1776 and the American colonies had just declared independence
from the British. But General George Washington knew things were not going the
Americans' way. When Gen. Washington needed someone to spy on the British, only
one young man volunteered. That man was Nathan Hale, an early American hero."--
Provided by publisher.

Identifiers: LCCN 2017934026 | ISBN 978-1-63440-282-8 (library hardcover) | ISBN 978-
1-63440-288-0 (ebook)

Subjects: LCSH: Hale, Nathan, 1755-1776--Juvenile literature. | Spies--United States-
-History--18th century--Juvenile literature. | United States--History--Revolution,
1775-1783--Secret service--Juvenile literature. | CYAC: Hale, Nathan, 1755-1776. |
Spies--United States--History--18th century. | United States--History--Revolution,
1775-1783--Secret service.

Classification: LCC E280.H2 D47 2018 (print) | LCC E280.H2 (ebook) | DDC
973.3850924--dc23

Photo credit: p. 29: Andrea Sprockett; p. 32: Courtesy of the author, Aaron Derr; p. 32:
Courtesy of the illustrator, Tami Wicinas

Map illustration by Joe LeMonnier

Printed in the United States of America

1117 1P CGBS18

Table of Contents

Chapter 1 — A Brave Volunteer

On September 8, 1776, the United States of America was only two months old. But already, things weren't looking good.

The thirteen American **colonies** had just declared their independence from Great Britain, and Great Britain wasn't happy about it. British soldiers had taken over Long Island, which is part of New York City. British warships filled the waters around New York. Many American soldiers were terrified that they were going to lose the war.

George Washington, 13 years before he would become our first president, was the **commander-in-chief** of the American army. He knew how serious the situation was.

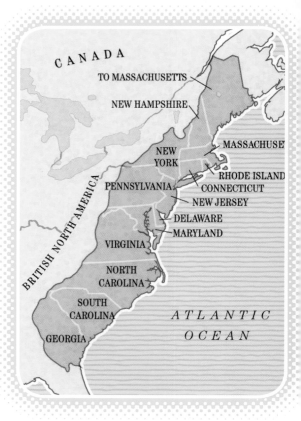

The thirteen colonies.

General Washington's only hope was to send a spy into Long Island to get information about the British Army.

How many British soldiers were there? And what were they going to do next? It would be a very dangerous mission. The spy would be surrounded by enemies. He would have to hide his true identity. If he was caught, he would be killed.

Thomas Knowlton, one of Washington's most loyal officers, called a secret meeting. He wasn't going to command anyone to take the job. He wanted someone to volunteer.

Only one person stepped up. "I will undertake it, sir," said Nathan Hale, a 21-year-old American soldier.

Four days later, Hale was behind enemy lines, pretending to be a schoolteacher from the **Netherlands**, secretly collecting information about the British troops. It was a good trick to pretend to be Dutch. There were thousands of settlers from the Netherlands in the colonies.

Patriots vs. Loyalists

Citizens of the thirteen colonies who supported the American Revolution were given names such as Patriots, Colonials, Rebels or Revolutionaries. Mostly, they called themselves "Americans."

But some citizens of the Colonies still supported Great Britain. They were called Loyalists.

A College Man

Pretending to be a schoolteacher was probably the easiest part of Hale's job. After all, he had just left a job as a teacher in New London, Connecticut, to join the war.

In 1769—seven years before he volunteered to be a spy—Hale left home at the age of 14 to go to school at Yale College.

Back then, not very many people went to college. In fact, at that time, there were fewer than 10 colleges in the thirteen colonies that would eventually become the United States.

And college was difficult!

Hale and his fellow students got up every morning before sunrise to go to church. Hale took classes to learn the languages of Greek and Latin. He also studied **philosophy**.

As he grew taller and stronger, Hale became a good athlete. He joined the Yale wrestling team and immediately became one of its best members.

After he graduated from college, Hale got a job as a teacher. He taught schoolchildren of all ages in subjects such as Latin, writing and math. During the summer, he taught a class that started at 5 a.m.

Best Friends Forever

One of Nathan's best friends at Yale was Benjamin Tallmadge. After leaving Yale, they stayed in touch by writing letters. (There was no email or texting back then. They didn't even have phones!) Benjamin signed his letters "Damon." Nathan signed his letters "Pythias." The Greek legend of Damon and Pythias is a story about two true friends who would never betray each other. Tallmadge would eventually became a soldier in the Revolutionary War, and he sent Hale a letter encouraging him to sign up, too. The date of that letter: July 4, 1775, exactly one year before the Declaration of Independence.

Hale was a happy man. But all around him, things were changing.

Many people living in the Thirteen Colonies were unhappy that Great Britain was asking them to pay **taxes** without giving them the chance to have a say in the laws that affected them. This led to the saying: "No taxation without representation."

"Why should we have to pay taxes to a government that doesn't care what we think?" people asked.

Let's Party!

Just a few months after Hale graduated from college, a group of **protesters** dumped a giant shipment of tea into the water outside the city of Boston, Massachusetts. The protesters were angry because of something called the Tea Act, which required Americans to pay an extra tax on tea shipped to the Colonies from Great Britain.

This event became known as the Boston Tea Party. But Great Britain was not in the partying mood. The citizens had dumped 342 chests of tea into the water. That tea was worth a lot of money!

Chapter 2

Hale Joins the Fight

For several years, Nathan Hale followed the news about the American Revolution from his home in New London. He had already joined a local **militia**, and he had been quickly elected 1st Sergeant, the highest rank of any new recruit.

In April 1775, he heard about the Battles of Lexington and Concord, the first real fighting in the American Revolutionary War. The British Army had sent soldiers to find and destroy American military supplies. But the Americans were ready for them. They had heard that the British were coming, so they moved the supplies to different places.

As the sun was rising in Lexington, Massachusetts, the first shots of the war were fired. Later, at a bridge in Concord, Massachusetts, more shots were fired. The poet Ralph Waldo Emerson called this the "shot heard 'round the world."

The war had begun.

A Big Decision

The people of New London gathered together at a place called Miner's Tavern to talk about what they should do. Lots of people showed up. This was, after all, a really big deal.

Some people thought that anyone fighting against Great Britain would be a traitor. Other people felt that they were being treated unfairly and it was time to do something about it.

But war is dangerous.

Should they risk their lives and join the fight? Or should they stay home where it was safe? Judge Richard Law banged his **gavel** on a desk, and the meeting began.

After much discussion, it was decided that the company of Capt. William Coit, made up of volunteer fighters from New London, would leave for Boston to join the fight the very next day. They had been training since the previous winter for this very thing.

Then, Nathan Hale asked for the chance to speak to everyone. As the local school teacher, he had earned a lot of respect from his fellow citizens. Everybody wanted to know what he thought about the situation.

"Let us march immediately and never lay down our **arms** until we obtain our independence," he said.

Marching To War

Hale didn't leave the next day with the rest of the militia. Instead, he worked hard to finish up his business at home. A few months later, he quit his job as a teacher and marched out of New London as a 1st Lieutenant with Connecticut's Seventh Regiment.

This meant he would be in charge of some of the other soldiers.

Hale and his men walked almost 100 miles to Boston. Once they arrived, they spent several months practicing so they'd be ready to fight when they had to.

But the winter was harsh and the men were running out of supplies. Some of the soldiers got homesick and wanted to leave. Hale did everything he could to encourage them to stay. He gave his personal supplies to some of them to make them happy. He even gave them some of his **salary**.

When it was all said and done, Hale's men were some of the best-trained soldiers in the entire army, and Hale was promoted to captain.

The Battle of Bunker Hill

Right before Nathan Hale left New London to join the fighting, the British Army had gained control of the city of Boston. When the British tried to spread their army out to the surrounding hills, the colonials were waiting. The British suffered heavy casualties. Even though the Patriots ended up losing this fight, the battle showed that the inexperienced militia could stand up to a regular army. The next spring, the colonists took control of Boston. It was their first major victory of the war.

Chapter 3 — His Secret Mission

On July 4, 1776, the thirteen colonies declared their independence from Great Britain. But the war was just getting started.

Great Britain focused its armies on New York City. So Hale's soldiers—and the rest of the American army—went to New York to fight.

British warships filled the waters around New York. Hale noticed that one of those ships, named the *Asia*, was guarding a smaller supply boat, called a **sloop**. Hale came up with a plan to steal the supplies.

It wouldn't be easy. The *Asia* was one of the biggest, baddest ships in the British navy.

Hale and a few of his men waded through the water in the dark. They saw a British soldier on the *Asia* standing guard.

"All's well," the guard yelled to his friends. He didn't see Hale and his buddies.

When the soldier left his **post**, Hale made his move. He moved quietly through the water, climbed up onto the ship and the steered the boat to shore.

He had stolen a British boat!

Knowlton's Rangers

In order to win this war, George Washington needed to know what the enemy was going to do. He ordered Major Thomas Knowlton to find the best men he could to carry out dangerous spy missions.

He called this group Knowlton's Rangers. And he wanted Nathan Hale to be part of his team.

For their most dangerous mission so far—sending a spy to Long Island—Knowlton needed a smart man. He needed a brave man. He needed someone he could trust.

"Without this information, our country is in great danger," Knowlton said.

Nathan Hale volunteered. "I think I owe to my country the accomplishment of an object so important," he said.

Hale needed a **disguise**. He gave up his military uniform and instead wore a plain brown suit. Then, he left his fellow soldiers behind and walked into enemy territory.

Dressed as a teacher looking for a job, Hale walked 50 miles north until he found a boat that would take him across the East River to the British side of New York. He had to be alert at all times. But he also had to act calm.

Collecting Information

Over the next several days, Hale made friends with British soldiers. The soldiers told him how easy it was going to be to defeat the Americans. At night, Hale wrote down what he had learned about the British army.

During his mission, British forces continued to advance, and George Washington's army had to **retreat**. Hale's friends were moving farther and farther away from him. At one point while Hale was in New York, a giant fire burned down a large part of Manhattan. Hundreds of people were forced out of their homes and into the streets.

Hale's mission was almost over. All he had to do was walk about 40 miles to Long Island, where much of the American army was stationed, and he would be safe.

But Hale stopped to eat. He met a man who appeared to be a friend. In fact, this man was Robert Rogers, a colonial Loyalist who had chosen to fight for the British. Rogers recognized Hale as a colonial soldier and figured out that he must be a spy.

Rogers told British officers about Hale. Nathan Hale was caught.

British General William Howe questioned Hale. After searching him, they found his secret notes tucked in his shoe.

The British had all the **evidence** they needed. There was no question what would happen next: The penalty for spying was death.

Chapter 4

The Final Hours

The next morning, Hale was forced by British soldiers to walk to the site where he would be hanged.

Moments before his **execution**, Hale was given the chance to say a final few words. **Historians** disagree on what exactly he said next.

In one of the most popular versions of the story, Hale said: "I only regret that I have but one life to lose for my country."

But most experts believe that Hale said something more like: "I am so satisfied with the cause in which I have engaged that my only regret is that I have not more lives than one to offer in its service."

You can see why the first version would be more popular. It's much easier to remember!

A Bad Sign?

Nathan Hale had a large mole on his neck. It was really a harmless mark on his skin, but when he was a child, his friends teased him that the mole was a sign that someday he would be hanged.

An American Hero

Frederick Mackenzie was a British captain during the war. He claimed to have been at Hale's execution. Mackenzie wrote about it in his diary: "He behaved with great **composure** and **resolution**, saying he thought it the duty of every good officer to obey any orders given him by his commander."

In 1783—seven years after Nathan Hale's death—the colonists won the war, finally earning their independence from Great Britain.

No matter what Hale actually said, there is no question about his role in American history. He is considered the father of American **espionage**, and he was the first American to be executed for spying.

The Hanging Site

Three different sites in New York City claim to be the spot where Nathan Hale was executed. Nobody knows exactly where it really happened. His body was never found. His family set up an empty grave in Connecticut.

In Memory of
NAThAN hALE
1755 - 1776

Lasting Legacy

At Yale College, now called Yale University, there is a statue of Nathan Hale. In 1985, the state of Connecticut proclaimed Nathan Hale the official state hero.

Dwight D. Eisenhower, the 34th President of the United States, said on the 200th anniversary of Hale's birth that Hale was "a supreme example of the willingness of an individual to risk death and sacrifice himself for the common good."

Even though he never made it back to Major Knowlton with his important information, Hale was exactly the kind of person every spy needs to be: smart, inspiring and brave to the very end.

Glossary

arms weapons and ammunition

colonies areas under the control of another country

commander-in-chief the person in charge of a country's army

composure being calm and in control

disguise something used to hide your real identity

espionage the practice of spying

evidence information that someone has committed a crime

execution carrying out a sentence of death

gavel a small mallet used by a judge to call for attention

historian an expert in history

militia a military force raised from regular citizens

Netherlands a country in western Europe

philosophy the study of knowledge

post a place where someone is supposed to stay

protester a person who publicly objects to something

resolution determination

retreat withdrawing from enemy forces

salary payment of money

sloop a small sailboat

taxes payments that must be made to the government

For More Information

Books About Nathan Hale

Olson, Nathan. *Nathan Hale: Revolutionary Spy*. Capstone Press, 2006.

Zemlicka, Shannon. *Nathan Hale: Patriot Spy*. Millbrook Press, Lerner Publishing, 2002.

Books About the American Revolution

Burgan, Michael. *The Split History of the American Revolution*. Compass Point Books, 2012.

Murray, Stuart. *DK Eyewitness: American Revolution*. DK Children's Press, 2005.

Places

Nathan Hale Homestead Museum, Coventry, Connecticut.

Nathan Hale Schoolhouse, New London, Connecticut.

City Hall Park Hale statue (one possible hanging site), New York, New York.

Index

About the Author and Illustrator

Aaron Derr is a writer based just outside of Dallas, Texas. He has more than 15 years of experience writing and editing magazines and books for kids of all ages. When he's not reading or writing, Aaron enjoys watching and playing sports, and doing pretty much anything with his wife and two kids.

Tami Wicinas has been drawing for as long as she can remember. She earned her BFA in Illustration at the Rhode Island School of Design. She is passionate about communicating story and emotion through the power of image and color. She currently lives in Berkeley, CA.